P9-DDM-894

OFFICIALLY
WITHDRAWN

James S. Thalman Chino Hills
Branch Library
14020 City Center Drive
Chino Hills, CA 91709

#2

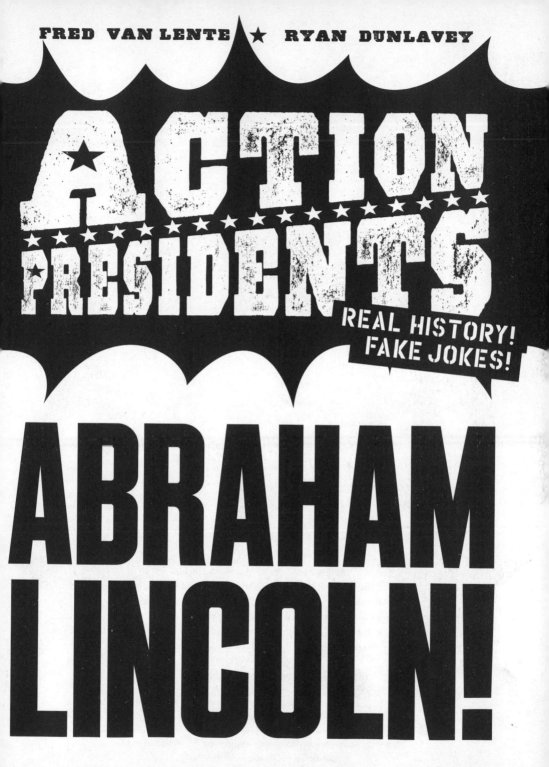

FRED VAN LENTE ★ RYAN DUNLAVEY

ACTION PRESIDENTS

REAL HISTORY!
FAKE JOKE$!

ABRAHAM LINCOLN!

HARPER
An Imprint of HarperCollins Publishers

Action Presidents #2: Abraham Lincoln!
Copyright © 2018 by Ryan Dunlavey and Fred Van Lente
All rights reserved. Printed in the United States of America.
No part of this book may be used or reproduced in any manner whatsoever without written
permission except in the case of brief quotations embodied in critical articles and reviews. For
information address HarperCollins Children's Books, a division of HarperCollins Publishers,
195 Broadway, New York, NY 10007.
www.harpercollinschildrens.com

Library of Congress Control Number: 2017954078
ISBN 978-0-06-239407-1 (trade bdg.)

The artist used Adobe Photoshop and Adobe Illustrator to create
the digital illustrations for this book.

17 18 19 20 21 CG/LSCH 10 9 8 7 6 5 4 3 2 1
❖
First Edition

For Gretchen, my super sis,
a great teacher and inspiration
—FVL

For Luke!
—RD

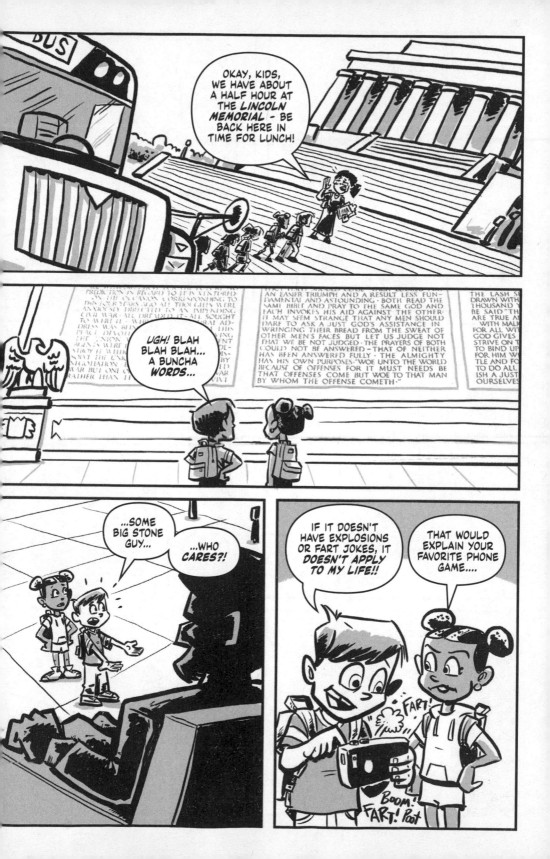

ABRAHAM LINCOLN WAS BORN IN 1809 INTO A COUNTRY *ALREADY* DIVIDED!

UNTIL THE *AMERICAN REVOLUTION,* SLAVERY EXISTED IN ALL *THIRTEEN* OF GREAT BRITAIN'S ORIGINAL COLONIES.

EUROPEANS BROUGHT ENSLAVED AFRICANS TO THE "NEW WORLD" TO DO THE WORK WHITE COLONISTS WOULDN'T DO – OR THERE SIMPLY WEREN'T ENOUGH WHITES *TO DO.*

BUT SLAVERY BECAME *MOST* IMPORTANT TO THE *SOUTHERN* PART OF THE COUNTRY. THE WARMER CLIMATE ALLOWED FOR *LARGE PLANTATIONS* GROWING RICE, TOBACCO, SUGAR, AND *COTTON.*

NY
CN RI
PA
NJ
MD DE
NORTH
VA
KY
SOUTH
TN
NC
SC
GA

These planters convinced themselves the only way to make a *profit* was if they used *slave labor.*

Slaves' lives were full of hardship and horror. They could be killed, abused, and sold away from their families for any reason. Under the law they were *property,* not people.

American slavery was inescapable. Anyone whose mother was a slave was *automatically* born a slave. It was nearly impossible for black slaves to buy or win their own freedom.

Northern states *outlawed* slavery during and after the American Revolution, partly because it wasn't that important to their economy and violated the ideals of freedom for which so many Americans fought and died.

Abraham Lincoln was born in Kentucky, a ***slave state***. His father was Thomas Lincoln, a poor white farmer who didn't own any slaves. It was hard for him to compete with large slave-owning plantations.

When Abe was just seven, Thomas moved the Lincolns to *Indiana*...

NORTHWEST TERRITORY

...part of the "Northwest Territory." This was land that had been owned by individual colonies and didn't become became part of the US until 1787.

The US banned slavery in the Northwest Territory. Southern states didn't want to compete with the new states selling tobacco and cotton.

THOUGH THE SLAVE STATES CHANGED THEIR TUNE ABOUT THAT SOON ENOUGH –

– FOR NOW, THEY WERE HAPPY BECAUSE THE NUMBER OF SLAVE AND "FREE" STATES WAS ABOUT EQUAL.

WHY DID BOTH SIDES HAVE TO BE EQUAL?

A LOT OF IT HAS TO DO WITH THE WAY OUR LEGISLATIVE BRANCH OF GOVERNMENT IS MADE UP.

350

CONGRESS

makes the laws of the United States. It is made up of two separate but equal houses:

The Senate

has a membership decided *by state*: every state gets *two* senators!

RI = 👤👤

TX = 👤👤

This is so *big* states can't get more power than *small* states!

To be a senator, you must be 30 years old, a US citizen for 9 years, and live in the state you're representing!

You vote for the senator from your state every *six* years!

Only the *Senate* can agree to presidential appointments and treaties with foreign countries (among other things)!

When the House wants to *impeach* a president, the Senate hears the trial!

WHEW!

The Senate voted *not* to impeach President Johnson... by one vote!

Sarah Johnston brought **books** with her from Kentucky – and Abe discovered a love of **reading** he'd have for his whole life.

Among his favorites were his stepmother's Bible and her collection of **fables** from the Greek poet **Aesop**, including:

The FOUR OXEN & The LION by Aesop

Aesop (620-564 BCE) began life as a **slave** but became one of the most beloved authors of the ancients.

A Lion used to prowl about a field in which Four Oxen used to dwell....

Many a time he tried to attack them, but whenever he came near, they turned their tails to one another, so whichever way he approached them he was met by the horns of one of them.

At last, however, they fell a-quarreling among themselves, and each went off to pasture alone in a separate corner of the field.

Then the Lion attacked them one by one and soon made an end of all four.

United we stand, divided we fall!

His *favorite* subject, though, was the American Revolution and its heroes.

When he was president, Abraham Lincoln would say he always hated slavery.

"IF SLAVERY IS NOT WRONG, *NOTHING* IS WRONG!"

Abe would plow fields, pull pumpkins, and *split rails* for fences. And he wouldn't see a penny of the money he earned.

This attitude was no doubt helped by *Thomas Lincoln,* who would often hire his son out to neighboring farmers. Any money Abe made would go directly into Dad's pocket.

Obviously, Abe and his dad did not really get along. Perhaps he never forgave Thomas for leaving him and his sister alone in the forest.

And Thomas seemed to prefer his stepchildren and their mother to the kids from his *first* marriage.

Still, many of Thomas Lincoln's *better* qualities rubbed off on Abe. Tom never drank or smoke, and neither did Abe.

Tom was by all accounts an amazing *storyteller* and a great mimic, and Abe absorbed those qualities from him.

ONCE THERE WAS A COLLECTOR WHO WAS JUST *MAD* FOR OLD REVOLU-TIONARY WAR STUFF....

Later in life, Abe invented a means to keep boats afloat even in shallow water with "inflatable compartments" – like a balloon!

He remains the *only* US president ever to receive a government *patent* for an invention!

New Orleans was a massive *slave* metropolis, one of the main buying and selling places for human beings in the United States.

His crew later said the sight of human beings auctioned off in public upset him greatly.

The flatboat returned to New Salem with goods to sell in the local general store, which Abe helped run.

BERRY-LINCOLN

He was notoriously trustworthy, once walking three miles to track down a customer he had accidentally overcharged by *six and a half cents!*

BOY! YOU REALLY ARE *HONEST*, ABE!

Abe was well-suited to being a *shopkeeper*. Back then it was the main *gathering place* for townsfolk. He regaled his friends for hours on end with his jokes and stories, just as *Thomas* Lincoln once did.

ONCE THERE WAS A *MAN OF DARING*, QUICK-WITTED, SELF-POSSESSED, AND *EQUAL* TO ALL OCCASIONS...

...WHO WAS ASKED TO CARVE A *TURKEY* FOR A *LARGE* PARTY.

HEY!

In 1832 the future wartime president got his first and only *military* experience when he joined the fight against the Sauk chief Black Hawk.

Abe moved to the state capital, Springfield, in the center of the state, to begin his political career just as a major political *movement* in America was starting.

ABOLITIONISM

was a movement by free African Americans and their white allies to ban – or *abolish* – slavery in the United States.

ALL MEN ARE CREATED EQUAL

ONE OF THESE THINGS ...IS *NOT* LIKE THE OTHER...

Frederick Douglass (1818-1895), *another* great author born a slave!

Though Abraham Lincoln always hated slavery – he was not an abolitionist, and often said so.

100

0

-100

He was a *moderate* – someone taking *neither* side.

AYE!!

Still, a resolution saying abolitionists were *bad* passed the Illinois legislature by a vote of 77-6...and one of those no votes was Abraham Lincoln's.

Like many Americans, Abe believed if slavery weren't allowed to move *beyond* the South, people there would *tire* of it and it would basically die of *old age*.

IS SLAVERY DEAD YET?

NO! NOT YET!! SSSHH!

To abolitionists, Abe's attitude was a *fantasy* – slavery would continue to exist in America as long as America *allowed* it to.

Many Illinois settlers, like Abe, were born in the *South* and fiercely supported slavery. Despite being a *"free"* state, Illinois had *"Black Codes"* preventing African Americans from voting or holding political office.

On November 7, 1837, Rev. Elijah Lovejoy, a white minister who published an abolitionist newspaper in Alton, Illinois, was murdered by a mob and his printing press thrown in the river.

Lovejoy's murder horrified Abe, and he warned in an 1838 speech at Springfield's Young Men's Lyceum (sort of a speaker's club):

"SHALL WE EXPECT SOME TRANSATLANTIC MILITARY GIANT TO STEP THE OCEAN AND CRUSH US AT A BLOW? NEVER!

"AT WHAT POINT THEN IS THE APPROACH OF DANGER TO BE EXPECTED?"

"I ANSWER: IF IT EVER REACH US, IT MUST SPRING UP *AMONGST* US; IT CANNOT COME FROM ABROAD.

"IF DESTRUCTION BE OUR LOT, WE MUST *OURSELVES* BE ITS AUTHOR AND FINISHER."

Though he didn't say it at the time, Lincoln's point was clear:

"UNITED WE RISE, DIVIDED WE FALL."

Abe was getting to be known as a *speaker* beyond simply a teller of jokes. He loved *words* and crafted his speeches with incredible care.

These skills served him well in his *other* career. State lawmaker was not a *full-time job*. It didn't pay all that much.

Abe was also a traveling *lawyer*, going from town to town to help farmers on what was called *"The Mud Circuit."*

When he came to town, he looked like an *uneducated man* from the country – and that's just what Abe *wanted* people to think.

"Any man who took Lincoln for a *simple-minded man* would very soon wake up with his back in a *ditch*," said one lawyer who faced him.

I FIND FOR THE *DEFENSE!*

WHA'...WHA' HAPPENED?!?

Abe's secret weapon was his way with *words.*

He won the case of a Revolutionary War widow who had been robbed of her husband's army pension when he described the hardships of *Valley Forge* so dramatically, the jury was in *tears.*

WHEN HE RETURNED TO SPRINGFIELD TO MEET WITH THE REST OF THE LEGISLATURE, LINCOLN SAT WITH THE *WHIG* PARTY –

NO, RYAN! NOT *THAT* KIND OF WIG! WITH AN *H*!

OOPS – SORRY!

THEY WERE NAMED AFTER THE POLITICAL PARTY IN ENGLAND THAT OFTEN OPPOSED THE KING.

THE AMERICAN WHIGS ROSE TO OPPOSE DEMOCRATIC PRESIDENT *ANDREW JACKSON*, WHO HAD A FIERY TEMPER AND BOSSY STYLE THAT LED HIS ENEMIES TO CALL HIM "KING ANDREW."

I WANNA BE ON THE $20 BILL! JUST 'CAUSE!

HE'S A KIIIIIIIIIIIIING!!

The leader of the Democratic Party in Illinois was Stephen A. Douglas – short in size, big in ego, known as the *"Little Giant."*

YES. I KNOW.

I AM AWESOME.

HEY, MAN! GET OFF OUR *MOVIE SET!*

The pro-South Democrats were much more *popular* in Illinois than the Whigs, so Douglas was one of the most powerful politicians in the entire state.

In 1838, Abe went to a party in Springfield and saw the Little Giant talking up *Mary Todd.* Mary was a rich young woman who was living with relatives in town and was also from Abe's home state of Kentucky.

GULP!

WHAT ARE YOU SAYING? I CAN'T HEAR YOU FROM UP HERE!

James Shields was the *auditor* of Illinois, meaning he had the job of inspecting how the state spent money.

Dueling – formal **combat** between two people – was **illegal** in Illinois.

So duels were usually held on a small island in the Mississippi River between Illinois and Missouri...

...so many, in fact, it was known as...

BLOODY ISLAND

According to the traditional rules of dueling, the person **challenged** was able to decide a bunch of things, like **where** the duel was fought and what **weapons** could be used.

Abe chose to duel using **broadswords**.

He also said they had to face each other in a twelve-foot-deep **pit** divided by a wooden plank **neither** could cross.

12'

All this would take advantage of Abe's height (he was 6' 4", Shields only 5' 9"), and long arms, which the blade would make even longer.

YAWN!

Abe could hit Shields without his opponent being able even to **reach** him!

Lincoln hoped that stacking all the odds in his favor would force Shields to **back down** and call off the fight...but he was **wrong**.

People waiting on the riverbank were horrified to see a **body** sent back in a boat!

GAHHHH! NO! THEY'LL HAVE TO TEAR DOWN THE LINCOLN MEMORIAL!!

OR BUILD ONE HERE?

Abraham Lincoln and Mary Todd were married in a small ceremony in the Todd home on November 4, 1842.

They moved into their first (and only) house in Springfield in 1843. It's still there, and you can visit it today.

For Mary this was a *huge* change in lifestyle: she had grown up on a plantation in Kentucky where she had *slaves* to do all her housework.

Now she had to figure out how to do that more or less on her own. *Four boys* were born here: Robert, Eddie, Willie, and Tad.

The state legislators of the Whig Party took turns running for the House of Representatives seat in the Springfield area.

A "House Seat" ... get it?

If the Whig won, he went to Washington, DC, to serve for two years. In 1846 it was Abe's turn, and he beat his Democratic opponent.

He arrived in the House just as the United States defeated *Mexico* in a war that began when Mexico's former territory *Texas* joined the US.

¡¡NO ES BUENO!!

TX

(Mexico's symbolic bird is an eagle too, from an old Aztec legend.)

Mexico claimed the USA started the war by attacking on *their* side of the Rio Grande.

¡AQUI!

HERE!

But US president, *James K. Polk*, claimed Mexico had attacked the US.

One of Abe's first acts in Congress was to demand that the president prove which country started the war and *where*.

POLK MUST SHOW US THE *EXACT SPOT!*

?!?!?

As you might guess, siding with America's *enemy* in a war is not the most popular thing for an American politician to do.

The White House just *ignored* Abe, and the other congressmen made fun of him *mercilessly*, naming him *"Spotty"* Lincoln!

AS NICKNAMES GO, I LIKED "HONEST ABE" WAY BETTER.

In the peace treaty, Mexico gave up a *lot* of "what joins mine."

¡NO ES BUENO!

The US gained what's now the states of New Mexico, Arizona, California, Nevada, Utah, *and* parts of Wyoming and Colorado!

This, of course, *immediately* restarted the argument as to whether the new states would be *free* or have *slavery*.

TEXAS WILL BE A SLAVE STATE!

AND *CALIFORNIA* WILL BE FREE!

WHAT ABOUT US?

Utah and *New Mexico*, largely *desert*, were useless for the large plantations that used slave labor.

THE *FREE* STATES SHOULD TAKE BOTH!

NO WAY, THE *SLAVE* STATES SHOULD!

But the slave states were increasingly alarmed by the larger population and industrial power of their northern neighbors. They wanted to add as much territory to their "side" as possible.

HOLD ON HERE! I'VE GOT AN IDEA.

LOOK, EVERYBODY! IT'S US SENATOR FROM ILLINOIS *STEPHEN A. DOUGLAS!*

WHEN THERE ARE ENOUGH PEOPLE IN EACH STATE, THEY CAN *VOTE* ON WHETHER THEY SHOULD BE SLAVE OR FREE!

LET THE *CITIZENS* DECIDE!

Then, in 1854, the US had to carve out two *new* western states, Kansas and Nebraska. Both were north of the Missouri Compromise line, so they should have automatically been *free* states, but...

...THAT WILL MAKE TOO MANY FREE STATES! WE'LL BE OUTNUMBERED!

I DON'T REALLY SEE THE PROBLEM HERE.

Senator Douglas wanted the *Intercontinental Railroad* to run through his home state of Illinois and needed *southern votes* in Congress to build it!

TELL YOU GUYS WHAT – THIS *NORTH/SOUTH* DIVIDING LINE – IT'S JUST *INK ON A MAP,* YOU KNOW? WE CAN GET RID OF IT!

WHAT IF WE HAVE THE PEOPLE *VOTE* ON WHETHER THERE'S SLAVERY OR NOT IN THOSE STATES, LIKE WE DID WITH NEW MEXICO AND UTAH?

I *LIKE* IT!

I DON'T *KNOW.* THAT MIGHT MAKE TOO MANY *SLAVE STATES!*

Douglas's plan, called the *"Kansas Nebraska Act,"* became *law* in 1854.

Pro- and antislavery settlers began moving to Kansas and fought with each other for control of the state government.

Stories of *"Bleeding Kansas"* filled the newspapers and inspired abolitionists to demand more and more loudly for slavery's immediate end.

Now that free and slave states had to compete with each other for territory, the relationship between North and South *worsened*...

...but it was about to get *worsener*.

The United States Constitution divides the government into three *coequal* branches:

Congress, the Legislative Branch, *passes* laws...

...the Executive Branch, headed by the president, *enforces* laws...

...and the nine justices of the *Supreme Court* decide if laws obey the *Constitution*.

Dred Scott was born a slave in Virginia. In 1846, after failing to buy his family's freedom, he sued his master's widow, or challenged her in court.

?!

Scott argued that since his master had taken him to the *free states* of Illinois and Wisconsin to live, it was *illegal* to keep him enslaved.

In the American court system, if you *lose* at one level, you can *appeal*, or ask again, to a higher and higher court –

– until you finally reach the *Supreme Court*, which is the *final* decider of what is and is not constitutional.

The Dred Scott decision, Bleeding Kansas, and other slavery-related problems added even *more* chaos to already *out-of-control* American politics.

The Whig Party *collapsed*, its members splitting along pro- and antislavery lines.

Antislavery Whigs and Democrats formed the *Free Soil Party*, which ran candidates on a single issue: no slavery in the West.

An anti-immigrant party best known as the *Know-Nothings* kept *mum* to outsiders.

WHAT CAN YOU TELL ME ABOUT YOUR POLICIES?

I KNOW NOTHING!

Then there was the *Constitutional Union Party*, which wanted to ignore *slavery* altogether in favor of keeping the nation *united!*

Elephant = symbol of Republicans since 1870s

Many ex-Whigs, Free-Soilers, and northern Democrats formed the new *Republican* party.

The whole situation disgusted Abraham Lincoln. He wrote a friend:

Though many issues faced the country and the state of Illinois, all anyone *cared* about now was *slavery*, and the candidates' positions on the subject were pretty clear.

The candidates agreed to a specific format for the debates:

One man spoke for one hour, the next replied for ninety minutes, then the first was allowed to wrap up for thirty minutes.

Then, in the next town, whoever went first last time went second, and so on for seven debates – over *100,000 miles* of Illinois territory!

Douglas used a couple tactics against Abe:

I HAVE KNOWN MR. LINCOLN FOR NEARLY *TWENTY-FIVE YEARS* – HE COULD BEAT ANY OF THE BOYS WRESTLING OR RUNNING A FOOT RACE –

– HE COULD RUIN MORE *LIQUOR* THAN ALL THE BOYS OF THE TOWN TOGETHER!

LIE.

First, he made Abe sound like the ignorant *hayseed* his own jokes made him out to be.

Of course, that could *backfire.*

YOU KNOW, JUDGE DOUGLAS'S STAND ON SLAVERY REMINDS ME OF A CERTAIN *MAN OF DARING...*

...WHO WAS ASKED TO CARVE A *TURKEY* FOR A *LARGE PARTY...*

Later, Douglas would remember:

"EVERY ONE OF HIS STORIES SEEMS LIKE A *WHACK UPON MY BACK....* NOTHING ELSE – NOT ANY OF HIS *ARGUMENTS* OR ANY OF HIS REPLIES TO MY QUESTIONS – DISTURBS ME.

"BUT WHEN HE BEGINS TO TELL A *STORY,* I FEEL THAT I AM TO BE *OVER-MATCHED*!"

...WITHOUT *FARTING!*

HA HA

HA HA

I SAY IT IS *BECAUSE* THEY WANTED SLAVERY TO *DIE OUT* IN TIME!

THEY KNEW – AS *I* DO – THERE IS A *CONTRADICTION* BETWEEN THE IDEALS AND MORALS ON WHICH THIS COUNTRY WAS FOUNDED AND THE PRINCIPLE OF *SLAVERY* –

– WHICH IS "*YOU* WORK AND TOIL AND EARN BREAD...AND *I'LL* EAT IT!"

CLAP CLAP CLAP CLAP CLAP CLAP CLAP

Today *we the people* directly elect United States senators. But in Lincoln's day, *state legislators* voted on who to send to Washington.

As Douglas and Lincoln crisscrossed the state debating, they were really campaigning *not* for themselves but for the men who would go to Springfield and elect *them.*

Lincoln did very well in the debates, and people were impressed by him. But in the end the *Democratic Party* still held the stronger position in Illinois.

ALL THE VOTES ARE *IN*, ABE....

THE DEMOCRATS HAVE A CLEAR *MAJORITY* IN SPRINGFIELD. THEY'LL SEND *DOUGLAS* TO THE SENATE, NOT YOU.

AH, WELL. SO IT GOES....

BUT MORE PEOPLE *VOTED* FOR THE REPUBLICANS THAN THE DEMOCRATS – SO YOU KNOW YOUR IDEAS ARE *MORE POPULAR!*

THAT *IS* GOOD NEWS – THANKS!

It was considered *bad taste* for a candidate to appear at the nominating convention. Abe waited for the results from Chicago in a vacant lot in Springfield, where he played handball and told *stories*.

Gen. ETHAN ALLEN (1738-1789), American Revolutionary War hero, co-founder of Vermont

se·ces·sion

(suh-sesh-shun) is the act of leaving a political state (like, you know, a *Union* of united states).

States had been threatening to secede since the first days of the USA, but no one had ever actually *tried* it before.

MASSACHUSETTS IS UP TO OUR EYEBALLS IN DEBT! WE WILL *SECEDE* IF YOU DON'T DO THIS PLAN!

WELL, MAYBE *WE'LL* SECEDE IF THEY *DO*! NYAH!

(previously on *Action Presidents: George Washington!*)

South Carolina argued that the states were "sovereign," meaning they really ruled themselves, because they preexisted the Union...so they could leave whenever they wanted!

DOINK!

By January 1861, five more southern states followed South Carolina's lead: Mississippi, Florida, Alabama, Georgia, and Louisiana.

THE NEXT MONTH, TEXAS ALSO JOINED WHAT BECAME KNOWN AS THE *CONFEDERATE STATES OF AMERICA* –

THAT MEANS IT'S PAPPY'S TIME TO SHINE!

WHAT ARE YOU – ERRKK!

I HEREBY DECLARE I AM SECEDING FROM THIS COMIC BOOK!

ACTION PRESIDENTS

JEFFERSON DAVIS

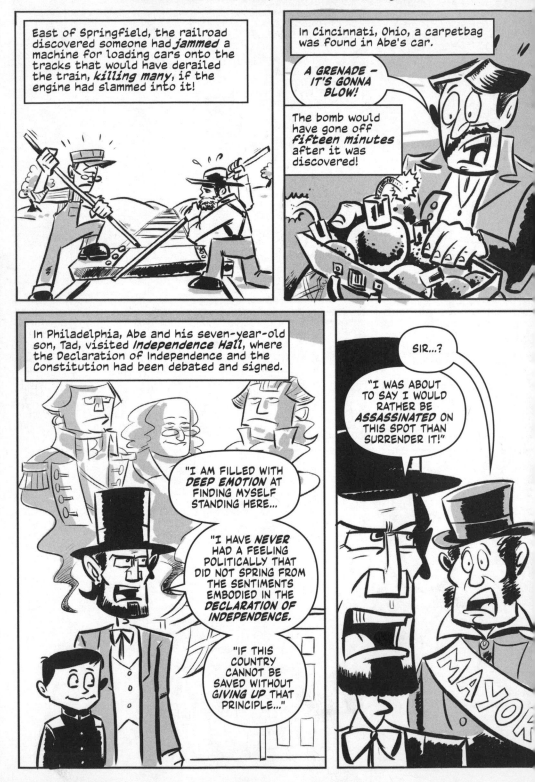

After the ceremony, the *outgoing* president, James Buchanan, dropped the Lincolns off at the White House.

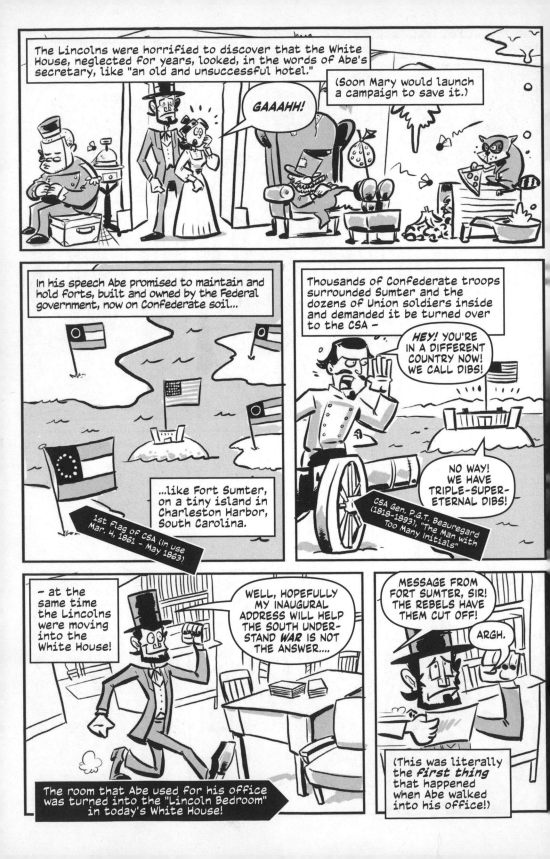

In April 1861 Abe decided to send only *food* to the trapped soldiers, making good on his promise that the North would not fire a *first shot.*

A lot of government jobs were open because they had been held by Southerners who left Washington to serve the Confederacy.

YOU'RE MY *BROTHER-IN-LAW*, BEN, BUT YOU'RE ALSO A GRADUATE OF WEST POINT, HOW'D YOU LIKE TO BE *PAYMASTER* IN THE UNION ARMY??

THAT... THAT'S GENEROUS OF YOU, ABE – ER, *MR. PRESIDENT.*

Benjamin Hardin Helm (1831-1863), married to Mary Todd's half sister

BUT...OUR HOME STATE, KENTUCKY, IS A *SLAVE* STATE...AND EVEN THOUGH IT'S STAYED LOYAL TO THE UNION...I DON'T KNOW IF I CAN FIGHT *AGAINST* SLAVERY....

IT WOULD MEAN A *LOT* TO ME TO HAVE YOU FIGHT BY MY SIDE, BEN....

WE'RE FAMILY!

LET... LET ME THINK ABOUT IT....

As Helm agonized over what to do, he ran into a friend of his, another West Pointer, *Colonel Robert E. Lee.*

Washington Monument, under construction (opens 1888)

WHAT'S BOTHERING YOU, BEN?

THE PRESIDENT OFFERED ME A MAJOR POST IN THE MILITARY.... BUT...

THE NORTHERN STRATEGY

played to the region's *strengths.*

The North had more factories, so it could make more *guns*. It had more *railroads* to get troops to battlefields more quickly.

And even more important, the North had more *free people.*

Their numbers could be replaced by *immigrants* from other countries who had come to the North for jobs that weren't available in the slave labor-fueled South.

Wars are often decided by who can *outlast* the other side.

Old "Fuss and Feathers" Scott developed the North's first plan for victory. He called it **"The Anaconda Plan,"** because the North would circle the South like a snake.

First, they'd blockade Southern ports with the Union Navy. Then they'd seize the *Mississippi River, which would cut* the Confederacy in two.

From these two extremes the Union would push in, strangling the rebels like a great serpent.

URRKK!

THE SOUTHERN STRATEGY

played to what they saw as their strengths, too.

The CSA planned to hold off Northern invasion long enough to be recognized by a *foreign government* that would make the USA back off.

(This, after all, was exactly how George Washington won the *American Revolution* – with help from *France*.)

Cotton was to the 19th-century American South what *oil* is to today's Middle East.

England and France depended on Southern *cotton* to make cloth in their factories.

The Confederacy was sure Europe would not let a Union blockade keep that crop away from their shores.

The Confederacy also planned to expand its borders by adding the still-loyal slave states... as well as conquering *South America and Cuba!*

All in all, the South's spirits at the beginning of the war were *high.*

Bred from an early age to think their culture was far *superior,* they truly believed, as one of Abe's aides put it, "that *one* Southern man is equal to *half a dozen* Yankees."

The South seemed to prove their superiority, too, after Fort Sumter, when the Northern public demanded Lincoln **strike** against the rebels **immediately.**

On July 21, 1861, Union troops marched on Richmond across the *Bull Run* stream.

Washington's elite people were so sure that they were about to achieve an easy and *final* victory that they gathered to watch the battle like it was an outdoor concert.

But the Union men were beaten back by a strong Confederate counterattack.

The North's hopes of a quick end to the war were swiftly dashed.

Still, Abe knew his history. He remembered George Washington's many early struggles during the Revolution.

He thought there would most likely be a long war ahead – and he made sure his generals knew to drill their soldiers to be ready for it.

"Old Fuss and Feathers" Winfield Scott was forced into retirement after the defeat at Bull Run, taking the fall for a battle he wasn't even *at*.

He was replaced by *George McClellan,* a young general with a royal bearing who was known as the "*young Napoleon.*"

He had a pretty *high* opinion of himself and believed the war and the country would be much better off if he was made *dictator*.

He agreed with Abe on the need for more training of the men, but he trained his men *so* well that he seemed reluctant to actually use them in *battle*.

ARE YOU ATTACKING TODAY?

NO! I NEED MORE TROOPS!

TODAY?

NO! WEATHER'S BAD!

DARE I HOPE? TODA—

LOOK HOW MANY *CANNONS* THE REBELS HAVE!

MY BEAUTIFUL ARMY MIGHT GET *HURT!!*

Lincoln doubted McClellan's constant excuses but wasn't sure because he didn't know much about military strategy.

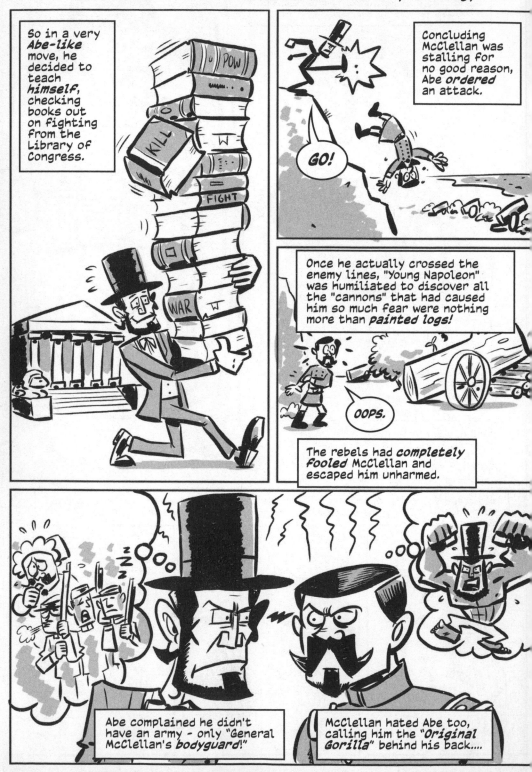

So in a very *Abe-like* move, he decided to teach *himself*, checking books out on fighting from the Library of Congress.

Concluding McClellan was stalling for no good reason, Abe *ordered* an attack.

GO!

Once he actually crossed the enemy lines, "Young Napoleon" was humiliated to discover all the "cannons" that had caused him so much fear were nothing more than *painted logs!*

OOPS.

The rebels had *completely fooled* McClellan and escaped him unharmed.

Abe complained he didn't have an army - only "General McClellan's *bodyguard*!"

McClellan hated Abe too, calling him the "*Original Gorilla*" behind his back....

In addition to his *personal* tragedy, the president also had to deal with the fact that the war was going *badly* for the North.

MR. LINCOLN! WHAT IS THE WAR ABOUT?

"MY PARAMOUNT OBJECT IN THIS STRUGGLE IS TO SAVE *THE UNION*, AND IS NOT EITHER TO SAVE *OR DESTROY SLAVERY*."

"IF I COULD SAVE THE UNION *WITHOUT* FREEING ANY SLAVE I WOULD DO IT, AND IF I COULD SAVE IT BY FREEING *ALL* THE SLAVES I WOULD DO IT...

"...AND IF I COULD SAVE IT BY FREEING *SOME* AND LEAVING *OTHERS ALONE* I WOULD ALSO DO THAT."

Noah Brooks (1830-1903), Abe's friend and White House reporter for the Sacramento *Daily Union*

Abe desperately wanted to keep the four slave states that *didn't* secede – Missouri, Kentucky, Delaware, and Maryland – from joining the Confederacy, so he kept his promise that he would leave slavery alone where it was.

WAIT! STOP!

Abe was forced to keep his commanders from freeing slaves in the rebel areas they took over, which drove abolitionists crazy.

In April 1862 Congress passed a law compensating Washington, DC, owners for *freeing* their slaves, achieving Abe's longtime goal to end slavery in the nation's capital.

OUT of BUSINESS

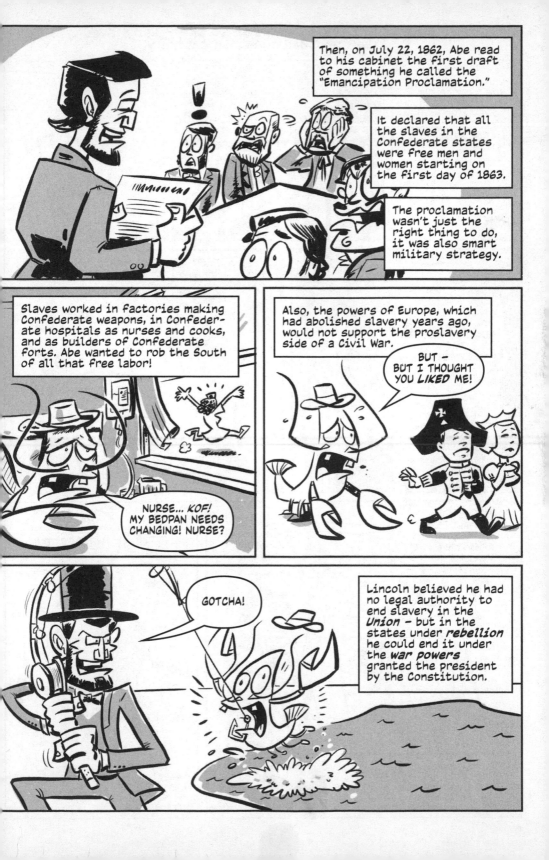

Then, on July 22, 1862, Abe read to his cabinet the first draft of something he called the "Emancipation Proclamation."

It declared that all the slaves in the Confederate states were free men and women starting on the first day of 1863.

The proclamation wasn't just the right thing to do, it was also smart military strategy.

Slaves worked in factories making Confederate weapons, in Confederate hospitals as nurses and cooks, and as builders of Confederate forts. Abe wanted to rob the South of all that free labor!

NURSE... *KOF!* MY BEDPAN NEEDS CHANGING! NURSE?

Also, the powers of Europe, which had abolished slavery years ago, would not support the proslavery side of a Civil War.

BUT — BUT I THOUGHT YOU *LIKED* ME!

GOTCHA!

Lincoln believed he had no legal authority to end slavery in the *Union* — but in the states under *rebellion* he could end it under the *war powers* granted the president by the Constitution.

What exactly would *happen* to the freed slaves was another question entirely.

– and his advisers said he must *wait* for a *Union victory* to announce it. Otherwise the government would look *desperate.*

Robert E. Lee gave him chase when he marched the Confederate army into still-loyal Maryland on September 3, 1862.

"SHE IS NOT DEAD, NOR DEAF, NOR DUMB – HUZZA! SHE SPURNS *THE NORTHERN SCUM!* SHE BREATHES! SHE BURNS! SHE'LL COME! SHE'LL COME! *MARYLAND! MY MARYLAND!*"

"Maryland, My Maryland" (1861) is *still* the official state song of Maryland even with those anti-Union lyrics!

Lee thought Marylanders would greet his men as fellow slavery-loving heroes – *instead* they cheered when Little Mac's Union troops arrived!

Incredibly, two Union sergeants discovered Lee's *battle plans* wrapped around *three cigars!*

TOP SECRET!

McClellan caught up with Lee at *Antietam Creek* on September 17, 1862, in one of the *bloodiest battles* in human history.

Men still fought in neat rows like they had for centuries, lining, shooting, reloading, and shooting again.

In the end, McClellan won, and Abe had his *victory*. He announced he was going to *sign* the Emancipation Proclamation on *New Year's Day*, 1863.

Predictably, the Confederacy *freaked out*.

A Union private wrote, "There is nothing (the Rebels) seem to feel so much, and care so much about, as to *lose their slaves*. I honestly believe that many of them would rather have us *kidnap their children*..."

TAKE PAPPIA AND PAPPY JUNIOR INSTEAD! *PLEASE!!*

In the North, not everybody loved the Emancipation Proclamation. Racist whites like Abe's own commander, George McClellan, *hated* it. He called it:

"AN *ACCURSED* DOCTRINE..."

"YOU WILL SAY YOU WILL NOT FIGHT TO *FREE NEGROES*.

"*SOME* OF THEM SEEM *WILLING* TO FIGHT FOR *YOU*..."

The Proclamation also allowed African Americans to join the *army* and risk their lives in *battle*.

But the Confederate Congress passed a law that any black troops would be *enslaved* or *shot*, and any *white* Union officer captured commanding black troops would be *executed*.

In October 1863, Lincoln signed a proclamation making Thanksgiving a national holiday. He wanted people to *give thanks* for all the Union's victories.

His proclamation declared that we would "set apart and observe *the last Thursday of November*" as a day of thanks for all one has.

THE TRADITION OF EATING *TURKEY* ON THAT DATE WENT BACK TO THE LEGENDARY FIRST THANKSGIVING BETWEEN NATIVE AMERICANS AND PILGRIMS.

UNFORTUNATELY! >*GULP!*<

Lincoln also started a *new* tradition, pardoning a turkey from the feast.

THIS I LIKE BETTER!

USA

Perhaps Abe got this idea from Tad's pet turkey, who freely wandered the White House grounds.

TAD, WILL YOUR BIRD VOTE FOR ME IN THE COMING ELECTION?

NO, PA — HE'S *NOT* OF AGE!

BALLOT

"– THAT WE HERE HIGHLY *RESOLVE* THAT THESE DEAD SHALL *NOT* HAVE DIED IN VAIN – THAT *THIS* NATION, *UNDER* GOD, SHALL HAVE A *NEW* BIRTH OF FREEDOM –
"– AND THAT GOVERNMENT *OF* THE PEOPLE, *BY* THE PEOPLE, *FOR* THE PEOPLE, SHALL NOT *PERISH* FROM THE EARTH."
SIT!
HAS HE STARTED YET? I HAD TO *GO!*
DANG!
YOU MISSED IT.
MOST OF THE LISTENERS WERE TOTALLY CAUGHT OFF GUARD BY THE SHORTNESS OF ABE'S *GETTYSBURG ADDRESS,* WHICH LASTED LESS THAN *THREE MINUTES.*
BUT IT SOON WOULD BECOME THE *MOST FAMOUS SPEECH* BY ANY PRESIDENT IN HISTORY!
WHY?

Because it made clear the Civil War was not really being fought over slavery, or state's rights, or any other specific issue but over the very idea of America herself:

It's the same reason George Washington was ready to ride out against the Whiskey Rebels during *his* presidency.

For thousands of years it was believed people were too stupid and scared to be ruled over by anything other than a small group of nobles and kings, by force.

Democracy is rule by the people - for the people - but by the laws that the people *themselves* create.

If some people can *ignore* those laws whenever they feel like it - then what's the good making them in the first place?

That's just proof that people can't rule themselves!

The Gettysburg Address says that the *hope* that the US provided to the world, that people could decide *their own* future, was too important to let go without a fight.

Still, Abe worried that a *future* government might pass laws overturning the Emancipation Proclamation and return *millions* to slavery.

Permanently changing the Constitution to outlaw slavery was the only way to prevent that — and extend the protections of the Emancipation Proclamation to the entire Union!

To make sure *mobs* couldn't change the government whenever they *wanted*, the Founding Fathers made sure it was very *difficult* to *amend*, or add to, the US Constitution.

QUIT, YOU GUYS! TOO MANY AMENDMENTS!

I'M GONNA BURST!!

We the People

To pass a *Constitutional amendment*, it has to be voted for by *two-thirds* of the members of the US Senate, House of Representatives, *and* state legislatures.

This was what the slave states that had stayed *loyal* to the USA had feared all along, but it was too late: the writing was on the wall.

ALL PEOPLE WILL BE FREE

>GASP!<

Public opinion had moved rapidly in Abe's favor since the Proclamation. After some false starts, the House passed the *Thirteenth Amendment* banning slavery *everywhere* in America on January 31, 1865.

NOOO — I'M MELTING... MELTING!!!

Completely fed up with George McClellan's *bad attitude* and stop-and-start battlefield tactics, Abe had made *Ulysses S. Grant*, the hero of Vicksburg, the head of the Union army on March 10, 1864.

BOOT!

Congress brought back the rank of *lieutenant general*, not held by anyone since *George Washington*, to give to Grant as a sign of their faith in him.

GO GET 'EM, "U. S."!

The "Anaconda" continued to constrict around the Confederacy. Grant's army chased Lee's throughout Virginia. Abe and Mary could watch some of the fighting from the White House roof.

Once, when an army surgeon standing next to him got shot, Abe kept on watching the battle until a captain had to yell at him:

UGH!

"GET DOWN, YOU FOOL!"

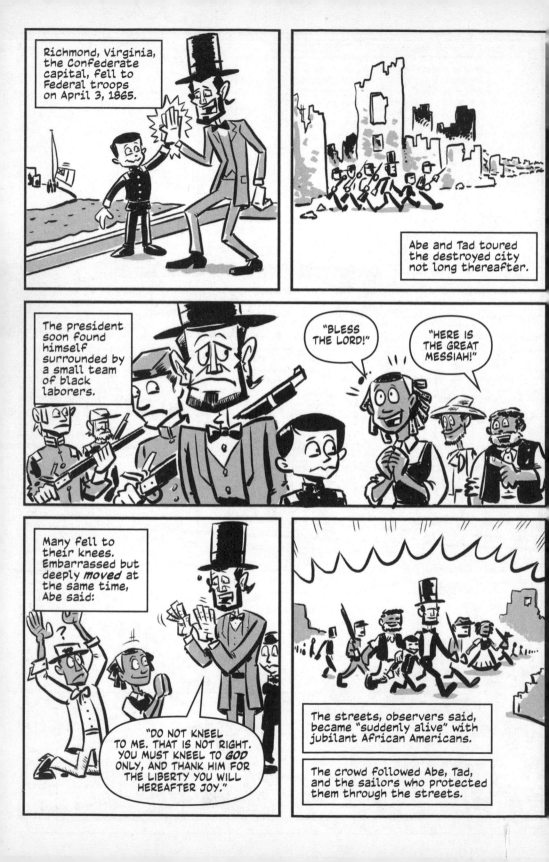

John Wilkes Booth had been a longtime friend to the Confederacy.

It was a much *sadder* train that brought Abe back home to Springfield for the first and final time since his inaugural train took him *to* Washington.

People lined the streets to watch the black-draped car go by.

In each city in which the funeral train stopped, citizens went to the tracks to pay their final respects.

Local mayors and governors were allowed to pass through the car and gaze at the coffin.

In certain places along the way, like in New York City, where his career as a national politician began, the coffin was taken to *City Hall*, where it could be viewed by the public.

THE NATION MOURNS

Abe's enemies wouldn't leave him alone even in death — *twice* grave robbers tried to steal his body out of his vault, but they were stopped each time.

SOON I WILL CREATE AN UNSTOPPABLE *FRANKEN-PREZ*! MWAHAHAHAH!

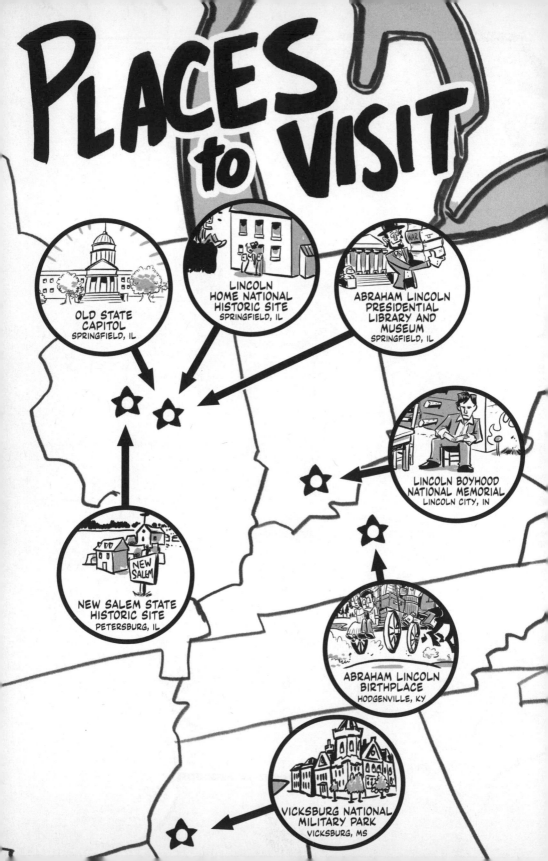

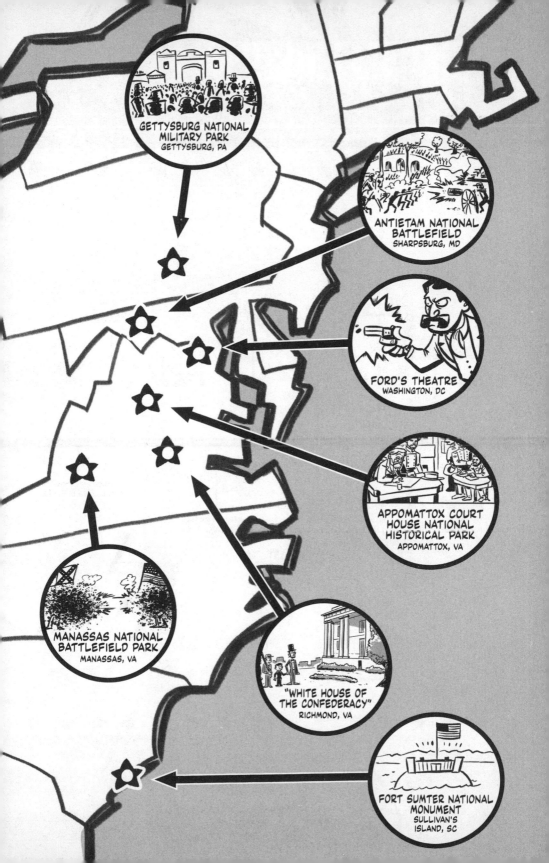

ABRAHAM LINCOLN

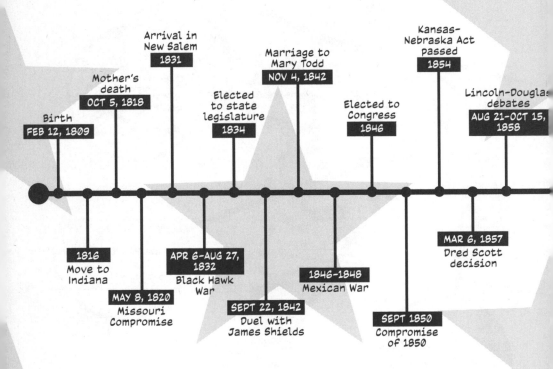

Birth
FEB 12, 1809

Mother's
death
OCT 5, 1818

Arrival in
New Salem
1831

Elected
to state
legislature
1834

Marriage to
Mary Todd
NOV 4, 1842

Elected to
Congress
1846

Kansas-
Nebraska Act
passed
1854

Lincoln-Douglas
debates
AUG 21–OCT 15,
1858

1816
Move to
Indiana

MAY 8, 1820
Missouri
Compromise

APR 6–AUG 27,
1832
Black Hawk
War

SEPT 22, 1842
Duel with
James Shields

1846–1848
Mexican War

SEPT 1850
Compromise
of 1850

MAR 6, 1857
Dred Scott
decision

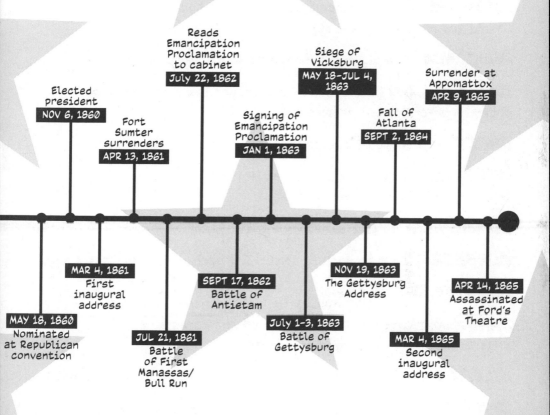

Reads Emancipation Proclamation to cabinet
July 22, 1862

Siege of Vicksburg
MAY 18-JUL 4, 1863

Surrender at Appomattox
APR 9, 1865

Elected president
NOV 6, 1860

Fort Sumter surrenders
APR 13, 1861

Signing of Emancipation Proclamation
JAN 1, 1863

Fall of Atlanta
SEPT 2, 1864

MAR 4, 1861
First inaugural address

SEPT 17, 1862
Battle of Antietam

NOV 19, 1863
The Gettysburg Address

APR 14, 1865
Assassinated at Ford's Theatre

MAY 18, 1860
Nominated at Republican convention

JUL 21, 1861
Battle of First Manassas/ Bull Run

July 1-3, 1863
Battle of Gettysburg

MAR 4, 1865
Second inaugural address

GLOSSARY

ABOLITION (n): getting rid of a practice or law, legally

ADVOCATE (n): someone who argues in favor of someone else

AMENDMENT (n): a change to the US Constitution
(there are 27 as of this writing)

ANACONDA (n): a big snake native to South America

BILL (VS LAW) (n): a draft of a proposed law that has to be
voted on before it can become law

CHORD (n): a group of musical notes played at the same time

CHRONICLE (n): a written account of history,
in the order in which events happened

COMMEND (v): to give somebody a task (formally)

CONSECRATE (v): to declare something sacred or connected to God

COUNTERFEIT (n): fake

DANDY (n): a vain, usually wealthy man who cares
a little too much about his appearance

DILEMMA (n): a difficult choice between equally good (or bad) options

DISRUPT (v): to change or destroy the nature of something

ELITE (n): a group of people in society seen as superior
due to wealth or status

ENDURE (v): to remain in existence

FLATBOAT (n): a cargo boat with a flat bottom (as opposed
to a curved hull) for use in shallow water, like in a river

HALLOWED (adj): what something is after it has been
consecrated (see above)

IMPEACH (v): to charge a member of the government with misconduct

INAUGURATION (n): a ceremony to mark the beginning of something (like, say, a presidency)

LEGISLATURE (n): the governing body of a country that votes bills into laws

MALICE (n): the desire to hurt or do evil

MEMORIAL (n): a statue or structure (or both) built to remind one of a person or event

MILL (n): a building that can grind wheat into flour

MILITIA (n): a military force of civilians raised to help out a country's army in an emergency

MIMIC (v): to imitate, usually for fun

PARAMOUNT (adj): the most important

PROPOSITION (n): a suggestion of a plan, usually in business

RELUCTANT (adj): "I don't really wanna"

ULTIMATE (adj): the best, or last, or both!

WIDOW (n): a wife whose husband has died

PATENT (n): a government license giving an inventor sole rights to an invention

PAYMASTER (n): the officer who pays soldiers of an army

PENSION (n): a regular payment a retired person gets from his former employer

PLANTATION (n): a really big farm

RESOLUTION (n): a formal expression of opinion by a legislature

SOVEREIGNTY (n): the authority a state has to govern itself

TREATY (n): a formal agreement between two or more nation-states

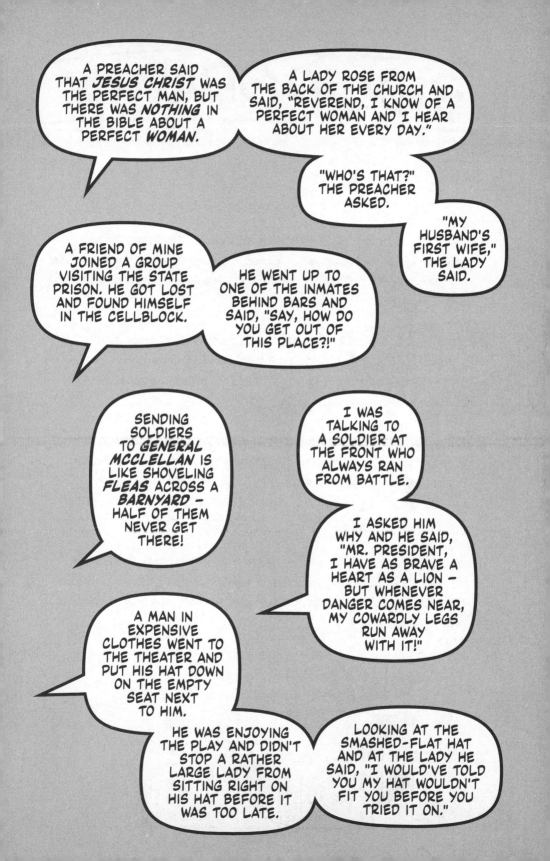

BIBLIOGRAPHY

Brookhiser, Richard. *Founders' Son: A Life of Abraham Lincoln*. New York: Basic Books, 2014. Lincoln's life as seen through his influences, from Founding Fathers like George Washington to the Holy Bible.

Dirck, Brian R. *Lincoln and the Constitution*. Carbondale, IL: Southern Illinois University Press, 2012. A very short but helpful look at Lincoln's legal mind, both as a practicing attorney and as president.

Eighmey, Rae Katherine. *Abraham Lincoln in the Kitchen: A Culinary View of Lincoln's Life and Times*. Washington, DC: Smithsonian Books, 2013. A super-fun journey of the author through Lincoln's life by the food he ate and prepared at each stage of the way, filled with recipes you can do yourself!

Goodwin, Doris Kearns. *Team of Rivals: The Political Genius of Abraham Lincoln*. New York: Simon & Schuster, 2005. A classic that is not just a biography of Abe but all his major cabinet members too.

Leidner, Gordon. *Lincoln's Gift: How Humor Shaped Lincoln's Life and Legacy.* Naperville, IL: Cumberland House, 2015. A great biography telling all of Abe's many, many, many jokes, gags, quips, and funny stories.

Lincoln, Abraham. *The Poems of Abraham Lincoln.* Bedford, MA: Applewood Books, 1991. Abe used his pen to write verse from time to time, including "The Bear Hunt," a verse of which is in our book.

McPherson, James M. *Embattled Rebel: Jefferson Davis as Commander in Chief.*
New York: Penguin Books, 2014. There are two sides to every story, and this tells of the challenges the president of the Confederacy faced to win the war and beat Lincoln.

Stashower, Daniel. *The Hour of Peril: The Secret Plot to Murder Lincoln Before the Civil War.* New York: Minotaur Books, 2013. As exciting as any fictional thriller, this tells of the Pinkerton detectives' endeavors to thwart the attempt in Baltimore to stop his inauguration train.

Doug Wead. *All the Presidents' Children: Triumph and Tragedy in the Lives of America's First Families.* New York: Atria Books, 2003. A great book full of interesting stories about all presidential kids, particularly Tad's and Willie's antics.

White, Ronald C., Jr. *The Eloquent President: A Portrait of Lincoln Through His Words.* New York: Random House, 2005. Abe was probably our best writer president, and this looks at how he composed his greatest speeches, from the Gettysburg Address on down.

ABOUT the AUTHORS

Fred

Ryan

Fred Van Lente is the *New York Times* bestselling writer of comic books like *Cowboy & Aliens* and *Marvel Zombies*. His previous funny nonfiction comics with Ryan were *Action Philosophers!* (named a YALSA Great Graphic Novel for Teens by the American Library Association) and *The Comic Book History of Comics* (which Fred's mom really likes).

Full-time award-winning cartoonist and part-time scout leader **Ryan Dunlavey** spends every day and most nights drawing cool and fun stuff for the world's most charming and attractive art directors. He's also the artist of the graphic novels *Action Philosophers!*, *The Comic Book History of Comics* (both with Fred Van Lente), *Dirt Candy: A Cookbook* (with chef Amanda Cohen), and the comic strip *Li'l Classix* (with Grady Hendrix). He can often be spotted with his wife, Liza, as they wrangle their two children on various adventures throughout the wilds of New York City.